# CRANMERE
## –THE FIRST DARTMOC

## Chips Barber

BA'

**OBELISK PUBLICATIONS**

## ALSO BY THE AUTHOR

Diary of a Dartmoor Walker / Diary of a Devonshire Walker
Beautiful Dartmoor / Beautiful Exeter
Torbay in Colour / Plymouth in Colour
Made in Devon *(with David FitzGerald)*
Dark and Dastardly Dartmoor *(with Sally Barber)*
Weird and Wonderful Dartmoor *(with Sally Barber)*
Ghastly and Ghostly Devon *(with Sally Barber)*
The Great Little Dartmoor Book / The Great Little Exeter Book
The Great Little Plymouth Book / The Great Little Totnes Book
The Lost City of Exeter / The Ghosts of Exeter *(with Sally Barber)*
Ten Family Walks on Dartmoor *(with Sally Barber)*
Ten Family Walks in East Devon *(with Sally Barber)*
Burgh Island and Bigbury Bay *(with Judy Chard)*
The South Hams / Dawlish and Dawlish Warren
Tales of the Teign *(with Judy Chard)*
Torquay / Paignton / Brixham
Around & About Salcombe / Around & About Seaton and Beer
Around & About Sidmouth / Around & About Teignmouth and Shaldon
Topsham Past and Present
From The Dart to the Start / Dartmouth and Kingswear

## OTHER TITLES ABOUT DARTMOOR

Under Sail Through S Devon and Dartmoor, *Raymond B. Cattell*
The Great Walks of Dartmoor / The A to Z of Dartmoor Tors, *Terry Bound*
The Templer Way, *Derek Beavis*
*For further details of these or any of our titles, please send an SAE to
Obelisk Publications at the address below, or telephone Exeter 468556.*

### ACKNOWLEDGEMENTS

Mr Brennan for Page 26 (bottom), Eddie Hain for Page 27, Mike & Hilary Wreford for Page 9, The Western Morning News Co. for Pages 18/20, Deryck Seymour for Page 11 (bottom), Paul Williams for Page 29, Peter Hodge for Page 31 (bottom), Jane Reynolds for drawing of box on Page 17, Mr Lennox Jones for Page 25 (top), Mavis Harriss for Pages 25 (bottom) and 26 (top). Thanks also to Anne and Dave Elford, Denis Mills, Mr Smith of the Local Studies section of Plymouth Library, the staff of Exeter's Westcountry Studies Library, Raymond Cattell and Eddie Hain.
Front cover photo by Chips Barber
Back cover map by Sally Barber

*First published in 1994
by Obelisk Publications, 2 Church Hill, Pinhoe, Exeter, Devon
Designed by Chips and Sally Barber
Typeset by Sally Barber*

# CRANMERE POOL
# – The First Dartmoor Letterbox

There is a lonely place, high on the roof of Devon, where the wind blows through the cotton grass, a wet and desolate land where birds and wildlife are scarce. That is, of course, apart from the 'lesser-spotted Dartmoor letterboxer' whose habitat is this kingdom of marshes, morasses and mires. It is here, deep in the watery wilderness, where many of Dartmoor's rivers are born, springing eternal from the bogs, that the evolution of that modern phenomenon called 'letterboxing' began. Misinformed moorwalkers who go to Cranmere Pool in search of a pool of any size, or expect to see a standard red 'letterbox' in response to that marked on the OS map, will be disappointed as the Pool is now an almost empty hollow, at all states of the tide.

James Perrott, a guide from Chagford (and also a Victorian hunting and fishing expert), thought the quaking lands in the vicinity of Cranmere Pool, high on the Northern Moors of Dartmoor, was the place to go to get away from it all. He would often take people in a pony and trap, along bumpy lanes, from the moorland-edge village of Chagford, up to Teignhead Farm. (This was long before any reservoir or forest, at Fernworthy, had appeared on the scene.) Above this point the terrain was impassable to any wheeled conveyance and walkers had to 'leg it' up and over the towering climb of Hangingstone Hill, one of Dartmoor's highest points.

Now if you have never been to this area you won't be aware of the 'delights' of walking in the Cranmere Pool district. It rains, so they say, on an average of 200 days of each year. The countryside in and around this legendary 'pool' is only gently undulating and so this combination of great volumes of rain and a sponge of oozy black peat, only broken by tufts, or tiny islands called peat hags, makes walking decidedly slow and the going extremely soft. This form of walking usually involves hopping from one tussock to another and it is common for even the most experienced of walkers to either overshoot or fall short of the mark. Even worse occurs when the 'solid' hag isn't as solid as it appears, giving way on impact! Another problem for the unsuspecting rambler is the inconsistency of the ground. Sometimes a harmless patch will see you immersed quite deep in the mire, whereas other places that look like they will engulf you, barely suck you in deeper than your ankles. A walking stick can be an invaluable aid and you should never consider walking alone in this type of wildscape.

Nevertheless James Perrott was undaunted by such terrain. On one of his regular quests to the Pool, in 1854, he placed a bottle there, for people to leave their calling cards. The next person could, if desired, collect these and make contact. However, in those early days, someone leaving a card there would probably have had to have waited a long time to hear from the next person reaching the Pool! Remember this was a wilderness, a Devonshire desert and walking for pleasure was to be more of a pastime of the future. Most folk had enough walking to do in their everyday lives and it was the last thing they ever wanted to do when they had time off from their workaday task.

Despite the excessive amount of precipitation falling on this elevated plateau, Cranmere Pool, in recent centuries, has been something of a misnomer as there is rarely any significant amount of water found there. However it is believed that there was a time when a substantial pool existed within the identifiable bank that had a circumference of about 220 yards. (William Crossing reckoned that it was precisely 192 yards.) Those with a similar mathematical mind have calculated that the waters of Cranmere Pool may well have been five to six feet deep then, simple surveying equipment or judgment by eye level suggesting this as possible.

The removal of peat from the banks of the Pool lead to a breach and the waters have drained away. But other theories of how the Pool came to be a pool in name only are numerous.

One story suggests that a miller living and working beside the West Ockment (Okement), in or near Okehampton, felt that the flow driving his machinery was insufficient. To increase it he punctured the perimeter of the Pool, thereby adding to the waters of the river.

Another variation is the story of the good shepherd who tended his flock on the high northern moors in the vicinity of Cranmere. When one of his flock fell in the Pool, he dug a hole in the bank to let the waters out and rescued his sheep.

Alternatively the Pool was emptied by the spirit of Benjamin Gayer or Gere, popularly known as Bingie (or Benjie) Gear.

This man held the municipal honour of being the Mayor of Okehampton five times in 1673, 1678, 1684, 1694 and 1700, the year before he died. But legend says that he was less than scrupulous and such were his sins that when he died he was doomed to become a dwarf and to empty Cranmere Pool, with a sieve! Dartmoor, with its excessive rainfall, made this an onerous, troublesome and toilsome task. Bailing away, morning, noon, night and day Bingie realised that here was an unending and impossible chore. So Bingie stopped and considered his situation. He looked around this watery wilderness and spied a sheep lying in a state of permanent somnolence with its four legs pointing heavenwards. Bingie seized the opportunity to use the carcass of the deceased sheep, covering the bottom of his sieve with its skin. Rejuvenated, he immediately set about the job of emptying the Pool. It is said that the added flow to the West Ockment was so great that it rolled down off the moor in a mighty flood and 'drowned the town over which he had presided as Mayor.'

There is this witty entry in the Visitors' Book on 4 April 1967, made by two people from Bristol, that is recorded thus:

*We feel it is our duty to relate to you what is happening, a happening which befell us while we were making our way here from Black Hill (Elevation 1916 feet) on approaching the proximity of the pool. We heard a scrambling noise in between the tussocks. Lo and behold it was a middle-aged dwarf dressed in traditional costume waving a sieve at us and crying in a shrill voice, 'I've done it! I've done it!' He then scurried off in the direction of Okehampton.*

In punishment Bingie has been condemned to haunt Cranmere Pool in the form of a black colt. The following excerpt appeared in the *Western Morning News* in July 1940:

*The Pool is said to be the abiding place of lost souls, among whom is numbered a certain farmer, so cunning that it took seven clergymen to secure him. When he was finally captured, he was transferred into a colt and delivered to a farm boy with instructions to lead him to the edge of the pool, slip off the halter and return without looking backward.*

*The lad, however, after obeying the first part of his orders could not resist the temptation to glance over his shoulder, and beheld the beast plunge into the depths in a fiery form. In return for his disobedience, he received a hearty kick from the vanishing hoofs, which deprived him of one eye.*

For those with the necessary staying power, I would recommend that you read the 1893 edition of 'Doidge's Annual' for it contains a poem that relates 'Cranmere Benjie's' story in a succinct sixty verses! For posterity's sake, and that alone, the last verse goes like this:

*Where once was a tarn on the lonely moor*
*The springs of Ockment near,*
*A darksome hollow now is seen,*
*On the hill-top bleak and drear,*
*And the gossips still the story tell,*
*How Binjie drained Cranmere.*

Benjamin Gayer died on 22 May 1701 at Okehampton.

But now we go back to the time when Queen Victoria was still on the throne. William Collier wrote this in the year of the Diamond Jubilee, 1897, and in so doing threw up yet another theory as to how the Pool was rendered almost dry:

*The original jar that was sited in the cairn at Cranmere Pool*

*Writers of guide-books are pleased to make much of this Cranmere Pool, which is now no pool at all, but just a small bit of bare black bog, greatly to the advantage of the living guides, who take tourists there to stare at a small bit of black bog, and leave their cards in a receptacle provided for them … It was a small pool years ago … but at Okement Head, hard by, a fox was run to ground, a terrier was put in, and by digging out the terrier Cranmere Pool was tapped, and has never been a pool since. So much for Cranmere Pool!*

Robert Burnard was a Victorian photographer of exceptional ability who had a knowledge and enthusiasm for Dartmoor that led him to visually record Dartmoor as he saw it on his extensive travels. Cranmere Pool featured in his thoughts. This is how he saw it many years ago.

*Surely no traveller ever reached it and was satisfied, for all he can see is a small heap of stones with a piece of wood stuck in the centre, situated in an inky-black depression of the everlasting bog.*

*Its inaccessibility is its charm; and the fun of the whole thing is to get there, and when there to find it …*

*A trip to Dartmoor should always include Cranmere in the perambulation, for no one can claim to be a genuine bog-trotter without having deposited his card in the tin box kept for the purpose in the small cairn in the pool. It can be approached on all sides, but most easily from the east; and a good point to start from is Post Bridge, proceeding through Hartland and the Grey Wethers down to Teign Head House, thence by White Horse Hill to Mute's Inn. The latter place sounds refreshing. It has, however, always been quite innocent of anything but imported liquor, being but a ruin of a peat cutter's small hut, which was built on this lonely spot some sixty or seventy years since by a Chagford man whose nickname was Mute. It is situated on the edge of the bog, and is one of the nearest points to Cranmere that horses can reach.*

*From Mute's Inn the course is Great Links bearing west, over about one and a half miles of ground which can only be traversed with a series of jumps. The bog is seamed and scored in all directions; and the wayfarer has to spring from tussock to tussock, or ignominiously flounder in a slough of black, greasy mud.*

In 1848 Samuel Rowe, vicar of Crediton, published his large volume *A Perambulation of Dartmoor*. It was added to in a revised and enlarged version in 1896. In it he paints, in words, the different faces of Cranmere country, first recording its unattractiveness and then saying

5

why it is attractive. If you have been there you will see just how accurate is his apparently contradictive portrayal. He wrote:

*In this immediate neighbourhood, quantities of turf are cut for fuel, and somewhat beyond the farthest point of peat-cutters operations, the approach to Cranmere maybe made on horseback without difficulty. The tourist will find himself on the borders of the vast expanse of boggy tableland, which characterizes the remotest and most inaccessible parts of the moorland wilderness ... The way [to Cranmere] in itself is toilsome, as you are continually plunging into the plashy soil; or, to avoid getting knee-deep in the bogs, or constrained to leap from tuft to tuft of the firmer patches of rushy ground. Nor is there anything in the surrounding scenery to cheer the wanderer who requires a succession of new and attractive objects to animate him in his progress. Here the image of 'a waste and howling wilderness' is fully realized. Glance where it may, the same slightly undulating, but unvarying surface of heath, common and morass, presents itself to the eye. Scarcely even a granite block on the plain, or a tor on the higher ground, 'breaks the deep-felt monotony' of the scene. Yet in this very monotony there is charm, for it gives birth to a feeling that you are now in the domains of primeval Nature, and that this is one of the few spots where no indication of man's presence or occupancy are to be traced. The few sounds that, at long intervals, disturb the brooding silence of the desert – the plaintive cry of the curlew, or the whirring rustle of the heath-fowl, roused by the explorer's unexpected tread – the sighing wind, suddenly wrapping him perhaps in a mist-wreath, or the feeble tinklings of the infant streamlets – for we are amidst the fountains of the Dartmoor rivers – are all characteristic of the scene; and wild, remote and solitary as it is, this central morass is thus associated with the richest, most populous, and loveliest spots of our fair and fertile Devon. Hence then we follow the mountain-born streams, along their devious course to the distant ocean, through green pastures and wavy cornfields.* I wonder what the Rev. Samuel Rowe's sermons were like?

Not everyone visiting the Pool had the same romantic notions. A gentleman, who signed himself 'A Visitor to Dartmoor', wrote to a leading London newspaper of the day, a letter which then featured in several provincial papers. He highlighted the problem of communications between the military using the moor for live firing, and the public who loved tramping over its great open spaces. This is part of his letter published in August 1893, in the early days of the moor being used for such military training. (Today August is a month when there is traditionally no firing.)

*Three of us started yesterday morning to walk from Gidleigh to Cranmere Pool, a well known centre of attraction, lying in the heart of the moor. They were firing from the camp at Okehampton, and from where we stood we watched the shot strike a hill some two miles away, while a random shell fell some half-mile off, causing us to change our direction, and approach the Pool from more protected ground. We heard the guns until one o' clock, when they ceased. At half-past one they recommenced, by which time we were in close vicinity to Cranmere, and we were alarmed to hear the shriek of the shells, followed by the thud, as they dropped within a few hundred yards of us.*

Cranmere Pool

*This locality is the watershed of the Moor, and the ground is seared by innumerable crevasses, down which the water finds its way to the Taw and Okement Rivers. In one of these fissures we took shelter, but were soon driven out by a shot striking the ground a few yards behind us, scattering the peat over our heads. None of these crevasses are, indeed, deep enough to afford the protection sought for, but only serve to render the ground exceedingly difficult to cross. To speedily get out of range was, therefore, impossible, and for half an hour – that is, until two o' clock, when the firing ceased – we were struggling over the broken ground under heavy fire, with the shells screeching in every direction.*

*Two fell within ten yards of us, a dozen must have fallen within fifty or a hundred yards, while a countless number more went tearing through the air above or to one side of us. If directed at the Pool, so precise was the fire that two shots while we passed its edge entered its banks. That none of our party were either killed or injured was a pure piece of luck, and yet we were in part of the Moor well known to be traversed by the public, at least five miles from the camp, with no sort of warning by way of flags or signals of any kind that danger was to be apprehended. We hope that the authorities will take care that the public shall be hereafter warned of their danger, or that the latter will accept the fact that the Moor has been rendered unsafe, and is to be given up to the military at the Okehampton Camp.*

At that time the Secretary of State for War was Mr Campbell-Bannerman, who later, in 1905, became Prime Minister. He replied to a question regarding what measures were taken to warn people going to Cranmere Pool from the direction of Chagford.

His response stated that the precautions that were in place were sufficient, that red flags had been flown at the usual places, that advertisements had been placed in the local press and that a shepherd, 'a keen sighted man', had been positioned at Cranmere Pool. But Campbell-Bannerman, ever the politician, went on to say that in view of this serious incident the general officer commanding the Western District would be instructed to take further precautions in future.

There have been further incidents on the ranges, one of the saddest of all occurring in 1958 for a family staying at Skaigh House, Belstone. From there Henry Whitfield, of Yelverton, took his 13-year-old daughter, Jennifer and his 15-year-old son, also Henry, on a walk to Cranmere Pool. They followed a ridge route, where possible, and reached the Pool at lunch time. Here they had planned to have a picnic. Whilst at the Pool another walker came and went and all seemed well with the world until they started hearing mortars exploding around them. Henry Junior climbed to a higher point in order to see what was going on and a mortar exploded just a few yards from him. Mr Whitfield got his daughter to a place of safety but his son died as a result of the severe injuries that he sustained.

Henry Whitfield felt that they had walked in full view of the surrounding area as they approached Cranmere. The fact there had been no firing when first in that vicinity was attributed to the troops also having their lunch break. The other walker at the Pool had said nothing about firing and was, presumably, also unaware of what was about to happen. Although money could not bring his boy back, Mr Whitfield successfully sued The War Office for negligence. A 'letterboxer' from Plymouth put out a series of letterboxes in memory of people who died on Dartmoor. Young Henry's was placed near Cranmere Pool and details of the tragedy were placed in the front of the visitors' book there.

In 1960 a youngster, who bent down to pick up a shell, lost a hand when it suddenly exploded and sadly yet another lad, 12-year-old James Gibbs, was killed near Belstone in 1987. The message is clear, take great care in planning before and during walks into these training areas and do not pick up metal objects. There are many ways of finding out about the intended firing, so always check before setting out to walk in any of the ranges.

There have been various attempts to clear such dangerous debris from the moor. 'Operation Eyesore' was a civilian undertaking in 1987 and dealt with all types of rubbish whereas 'Operation Tidywyvern' was a military clean up in 1989 to remove all manner of potentially lethal objects from the Dartmoor firing ranges in the March and April of that year prior to the main influx of walkers and visitors.

But despite the dangers the Pool's reputation grew and over the years the challenge to get there was taken up by ever-increasing numbers. Throughout the twentieth century thousands of intrepid ramblers, every year, have made the pilgrimage into the middle of this upland morass. Those who have braved the elements and found their way over the fen, down through the years, would have encountered various receptacles for their cards. William Crossing, that most celebrated of Dartmoor writers, wrote this in one of his numerous books …

*In the pool is a little heap of stones, and in a hollow in this is kept a small tin box – I have seen two there – for the reception of the cards of visitors. The spirit of vandalism, unfortunately but too prevalent, may have intruded itself here, but, on the whole, the contents of the boxes seem to be well respected. I can at all events affirm that I have found names there – my own among others – which had been left at the pool several years before.*

In 1889 (some reports quote 1887 and others 1903) a tin box replaced the glass jar that had been placed in the cairn, but by 1905 there was need of an upgrade and with it a means by which the increasing number of Cranmereans could record their attendance at this university of the wilderness. Mr H. P. Hearder, of Plymouth, asked the Duchy authorities for permission and they agreed, whilst declining any responsibility for it. They advised Mr Hearder that it should be made in such a way that it could not be removed easily. The container was a zinc box with double corners and 'stout angles.' For an outlay of seven shillings, Cranmere was now endowed with a receptacle that must have worked well as anyone who inspects those early Visitors' Books at Plymouth Library will see that they are in better condition than those of more recent decades.

According to some sources the first post-box did not arrive on the scene until 1912, the year the *Titanic* went down. Other reports plump for 1910, but it's so long ago it hardly matters!

As can be imagined, getting it there to install it was no easy matter. Almost inevitably the box was made in Chagford, the moorland town that had yielded the great Perrott who had installed the first receptacle. This time the box was the handiwork of J. W. F. Rowe who, in a life time of Dartmoor walking, visited the Pool and his box no less than 165 times! To get it to Cranmere a sled was employed and the box was taken there via Huggaton Cut. Nevertheless Perrott's cairn remained at the Pool for a few years more.

The nature of the countryside around Cranmere is such that walkers are strongly advised not to walk in solo fashion as a broken ankle or leg could have quite disastrous consequences. Although few people, to our knowledge, have ridden a horse all the way to the Pool there are a few instances where people have managed to ride within about a hundred yards of it. George Collier took advantage of exceptionally dry conditions in 1890 to ride to the Pool. Fifteen years later on 28 May 1905 John and Sydney Worden visited Cranmere Pool with two ponies and three dogs. The entry in the book is a little unusual for, if it is correct, it reveals that these men conquered Cranmere at nightfall and on horseback. According to the good book they arrived at the pool at 10.30 pm, having left Bridestowe at 6.30 pm. There is another entry for the same day, written afterwards, that appears to be recorded at an earlier time, so they probably mistook AM for PM.

In the 1950s the late Eric Hemery, another celebrated Dartmoor writer, worked as a guide out of Chagford. He escorted, on horseback, a client, in 1957, to within 100 yards and has published photos of him, his guest and their two ponies at Cranmere Pool. He rode from Gidleigh via Wild Tor, Bow Combe, Taw Ford and Huggaton Cut carefully picking out the firmest and most even route available. Only a real Dartmoor expert and accomplished rider ought to consider such a potentially difficult hack.

The letterbox is marked on Ordnance Survey maps and to visit it should be a compulsory part of any Dartmoor devotee's education. However, anyone wishing to visit the Pool, perhaps for the first and only time, only armed with The Dartmoor Tourist Map (one inch to the mile or 1:63 360) should note that the name is shown but the precise location is not marked with a dot! In practical terms it means that you will, like many thousands before you, probably search in vain as the name on the map covers several hundred yards of featureless country. Aim left of the name and find the Pool just south of the head of the West Okement! A scale of 1:25 000 is recommended for then nothing should go wrong ... Salvation lies in the shape of the O/S Outdoor Leisure Map No 28 that covers Dartmoor. But take a tip from me, don't open it up to its full extent on a windy day near Cranmere for you might end up flying over the Pool!

Cranmere is well worth visiting, a sentiment shared by Royalty. In 1921 expert guide, Jim Endicott, took Edward, Prince of Wales, Sir Walter Peacock, Admiral Sir Lionel Halsey, and

Lord Clinton to the Pool. They made their approach from Fernworthy and were en route to the peatworks at Rattlebrook, to the west. All the while a speck in the distance got ever closer to them and when the speck was close enough it was found to be a press photographer in hot pursuit of the Royal party. However his equipment was heavy, the conditions underfoot difficult and the weather misty and clingingly damp.

The future Edward VIII, when asked to pose for the obligatory photo there replied, whilst appreciating the photographer's mighty struggle with heavy equipment in those pre-telescopic days, "You deserve fifty photos for carrying this ten miles!" One of the party produced a hip flask and the dedicated photographer was revived!

The Pool has also attracted all the great Dartmoor writers whose books populate the shelves of our houses and whose names appear in the various Visitors' Books – an impressive list that includes William Crossing, Beatrice Chase, Ruth St Leger-Gordon, Douglas Gordon, Eric Hemery, Eden Philpotts, Raymond B. Cattell, Harry Starkey, Vian Smith, Deryck Seymour, John Robins, Brian Carter, Jeffrey Malim, Terry Bound (and Chips Barber?).

William Crossing made this journey to Cranmere and featured it in his book *Amid Devonia's Alps*.

*It was a bright morning in the summer of 1881 when I set out with a companion from the town of Moretonhampstead for a ramble on the moor, with the intention of visiting Cranmere Pool in the course of our wandrings. My companion had never been on the north quarter before, and I was anxious to show him some objects of interest there, so not desirous of losing any time, we stepped out briskly towards the moor. This we entered at the gate near Metherell, a farm just on its borders, and proceeded towards Fernworthy, to which a road leads. We did not, however, keep to this, but made a detour to the south of it, and wending around regained it where it crosses the South Teign, and not very far from Fernworthy farmhouse.*

*Close to this bridge, which is a modern erection, is an old clapper bridge, consisting of one immense stone, which I have found to measure ten feet four inches in length, having a width of three feet ten inches, and a thickness of about a foot. The buttresses, which are rather high, are built of rough, un-hewn stones. It is very interesting, and a good specimen of a single stone clapper.* [It now lies beneath the waters of Fernworthy Reservoir, except during droughts!]

*Passing on we soon reached Fernworthy, an ancient moor farm, lying just within the bounds of the forest* [Not the Fernworthy Forest of today but the ancient Forest of Dartmoor] *and in its eastern quarter ... By its grey old walls grow some fine trees, affording in summer a cool and grateful shade, when the noonday sun blazes full upon the hot and thirsty heath...*

*Leaving Fernworthy behind us we passed through the gate at the top of the lane that runs by the house, and emerged once more upon the commons, shortly reaching the fine circle of upright stones near by ... Proceeding up the slope we made our way to the gate in the new-take wall, and descended by a rough track to an ancient clapper bridge over the North teign, and not far from the solitary Teign Head Farmhouse ...*

*The bridge is a very good specimen, although not so interesting as some others on the moor. The imposts are not nearly so large as those at Post Bridge or Belleford. There they consist of slabs of granite of immense size ...*

*Teign Head farm house is one of the most solitary on all Dartmoor, being far removed from any other habitation, and adjoining some of the wildest parts of the moor. A stranger coming across its existence would certainly be surprised at coming across a dwelling in such a remote spot. Its situation on such a high part of Dartmoor, although it is fairly well sheltered by rising ground around it, must have exposed it to the pitiless severity of many a winter storm; but the old house looks none the worse for the fury of the mountain winds which have beat against it, its grey walls seeming to bid defiance to the attacks of the elements.*

*Leaving the farm-house at some distance on our left hand, we mounted the slope which raises from the river, and made our way across the new-take to White Horse Hill, an eminence from whence a goodly view of the surrounding moor is to be obtained. From here we passed onward to East Dart Head, where we called a halt, and rested awhile at my Chair. The day was a very hot one, and we were not sorry to repose for a short time among the heather. After having refreshed ourselves we arose and struck out over the bogs for Cranmere Pool, which, as I have already observed, is but a short distance from the springs of the East Dart.*

The moor has changed in many ways since Crossing roamed it, the major changes being  the great coniferous forests that enveloped great areas of open moorland and the installation of reservoirs to serve the ever-growing population and demands of lowland Devon. Hill farming too has lost its appeal for both social and financial reasons and Teignhead Farm is little more than a heap of rubble.

Crossing loved the wildest and remotest tracts of land and it is fitting that his own memorial is one of the other 'letterboxes' shown on OS maps. Ducks Pool (also written as Duck's Pool or Ducks' Pool) is the southern moor's equivalent of Cranmere Pool and a small plaque, cast at the Upton Foundry in Torquay, measuring $8^1/_2$ inches x $6^1/_2$ inches set on a large boulder, carries this inscription: "In memory of William Crossing, author of many inspiring books on Dartmoor, whose guide is a source of invaluable information to all lovers of the moor. Died 3rd Sep 1928 aged 80." His books, particularly his *Guide to Dartmoor* have immortalised his love and knowledge of Dartmoor. Dr J. W. Malim was a founder member of Dobson's Moormen and it was his idea to place a box at Ducks Pool, although it was a group of other people from St Marychurch who turned the notion into reality. Having gained permission from The Duchy, the letterbox was opened on 23 October 1938 but not without quite a struggle …

The weather was wet and misty, one of the wettest of that year, when the letterbox-building party set out from Nun's Cross Farm to walk the two miles to Ducks Pool. Harry Franks carried a sack of sand and cement on his back, only to get to the 'pool' and remember that there was plenty of sand there already – rather like taking coals to Newcastle!

A. J. Patty supplied a zinc box that served the required purpose for twelve years until Dr Malim provided a copper one, to replace it, in 1950. Mr W. F. Ozzard supplied the rubber stamp and Mr Aaron Luxton, a builder, provided the teak box to house the items. Along with Dr Malim, two of the Plymouth-based 'Dobson's Moormen', Collins and Carpenter also attended the installing and initiation ceremony on a Sunday that was certainly wet enough for Ducks! The photo shown here was taken in October 1947 and shows author and historian, Deryck Seymour, at Ducks Pool. With him was his dentist, far right, and his dentist's brother, centre. Please note the smart attire worn by walkers in those days when collar and tie were the norm, particularly when visiting a shrine such as this.

Dr Malim, who was a highly respected walker and Dartmoor writer, had his ashes scattered on his favourite hill, Rowdon, near Widecombe, where a small plaque is attached to the rocks on the summit of this hill.

There have been even greater literary fellows who have made their pilgrimage to Cranmere and these include Charles Kingsley, Charles Dickens and R. D. Blackmore, all greatly influenced in their writings by their times in Devon. Charles Causley is recorded as having visited on 5 May 1935 with Launceston Hiking Club and wrote in the Visitors' Book, *Water, water everywhere and not a drop to drink!*

Another fine fellow who traipsed across the wilderness, and was no doubt heavily influenced by his sojourn to the Pool, was Henry Williamson (1895-1977). H. W's visit was in 1926, the year before his famous *Tarka the Otter* was published. Like every great novelist his research was painstaking in order to get the right mood, atmosphere and setting for his work. So we get from him in Chapter 11 of *Tarka*, these words that so many have read, the whole world over, from North Devon to North Dakota and from Okehampton to Oklahoma!

*Bogs and hummocks of the Great Kneeset were dimmed and occluded; the hill was higher than the clouds… Broken humps, rounded with grey moss and standing out of the maze of channers, made the southern crest of the hill. In the main channer, below banks of crumbling peat, lay water darkstained and almost stagnant. Tarka ran past a heap of turves, set around the base of a post marking Cranmere Tarn, now empty, whither his ancestors had wandered for thousands of years.*

Beatrice Chase was an 'eccentric' lady, born in 1874, and many are the folk I have encountered with unusual tales to tell of her bizarre behaviour. She is buried, having died two days short of her 81st birthday in June 1955, in Widecombe's churchyard with a cross that bears 'Beatrice Chase' on one side and 'Katherine Parr', her real or birth name, on the other. This is a letter that she posted from Cranmere Pool to the *Devon & Exeter Gazette,* which they published on 2 October 1929. Good job her message wasn't urgent! Don't lay too much store in her directions and distances …

*Cranmere, September 24th 1929*

*I am posting this in Bingie's box. On Sunday came a ring, and, as both my men were off duty, I answered the bell. A charming man wanted to know the way to Totnes, after which we were soon engrossed in an enthralling conversation about Cranmere. I told him I was going to-day. He had done the same route last Sunday and had made a splendid little map which he graciously left with me for my guidance. Life is full of these fairy tales.*

*To-day's route was via the Artillery road from Okehampton. A car can be driven to within two miles and the road is struck at the camp, which is about two miles from Okehampton. It leads through a moor gate, across a stream and thence due south to the first bomb shelter where the car must be left. Soon after crossing the stream, an inviting looking road branches off to the left, but it is a snare, as it is full of shell holes. Keep straight to the shelter. There dismount, and steer for the next bomb-proof shelter, passing a cart track on the right and not turning down it. This cart track does lead into Cranmere by a large half circle and a longer distance. By heading in a straight line from shelter No. 2. you make a bee line for the spot. Half way between Cranmere and the shelter are four large grass hummocks which are a landmark. Hangingstone Hill is on the left skyline about two miles distant from Cranmere. In wet weather, the right cart track, though longer, is drier walking, the bee line track being 'squishy.'*

*In my last article I mentioned a nice man with a party of girls who kindly snapped me. Well, of course, this nice man was a friend of the nice visitor's. Life is full of these fairy tales. It seems, after leaving his car, his party could not even then find Cranmere, though so near it, and were guided to it by my white sunshade which I had taken in lieu of a hat. In my article in this paper, September 12th, I mention posting lots of cards in Bingie's box on September 7th. Those cards were collected the next day, Sunday, the 8th, and were postmarked Plymouth, 6.30 a.m. September 9th. I fastened my cards together with an elastic band, and on top of my little pile I put a signed picture postcard of myself addressed, 'To the Right Hon. Lady or Gentleman who kindly posts this mail, a token of gratitude from the writer.'*

*Frightfully conceited of me to think anyone would care for my signed picture, of course, but the British public is so sweet about my silly schemes and plays up to them so nobly! My visitor told me that his friend saw my pile and the inscribed picture in Bingie's box, and wanted it so dreadfully that he had a sharp struggle with himself and remarked bitterly 'That's always the reward for being honourable.' It is an unwritten code at Cranmere never to collect the mail the same day. So the right honourable gentleman went away, empty-handed, and we do not know who got the coveted card.*

*He does not know that his friend has told me, so to-day, I have posted another card, a signed portrait, in Bingie's box, addressed to the gentleman, and bearing the inscription 'To the Still More Right Honourable Gentleman, who played the game on September 7th, with admiring greetings from 'My Lady of the Moor.' We are simply squirming with excitement to think what he will say when he gets that card. His friend had solemnly sworn not to say he has even seen me so that the shock may be perfect. If the friend had not wanted to know the way to Totnes, if I had not been in, if my men had been on duty – but life is full of these fairy tales. And if there were any doubt as to the standard of honour in England, observation of Bingie's post-box and the way those mails are run by the British public would set this doubt at rest for good.*

One may presume then this was a fairy tale – or three – with a happy ending, a few people better off with a not too 'squishy' photo of the 55-year-old authoress.

Miss Chase refers to the bomb shelters along the Artillery Road and although the military have designated them with OP (Observation Post) numbers, most folk refer to them as 'Splinter Proofs'. But who are we to argue, for her first book *The Heart of the Moor*, published in 1914, sold a staggering 80,000 copies!

OP15, on the peak of the Artillery Road, is the most mentioned 'Splinter Proof', one of about 22 such refuges built by the armed forces for shelter when the bullets are flying. They were established by the military and resulted in quite a few raised eyebrows when they first appeared.

Originally they were built of bulk timber and their squat cube shape were distinct warts on the face of the moor, out of keeping with the surroundings and out of favour with those who saw them as the worst blots on the landscape. To appease those whose nerve ends had been frayed by these intrusions it was decided to encase them in stone, and so they were stone-clad to help them blend in with the moor. Although most will refer to them by their numbers, there are those who will recall that they had originally been given names like 'Kelly', 'Middleton' and 'Saunders'. These were bestowed on these surface bunkers because these were the names of the men who built them. OP15 is the nearest to Cranmere Pool and one that has been a fond landmark, a king among among Splinter Proofs, despite its lack of obvious aesthetic beauty.

The builders were paid only from the moment when they passed through Moor Gate, beside Okehampton Camp, an unusual form of clocking on. One can almost imagine them rushing frantically to get through the gate then to take several minutes, now on their employers' time, to recover from the race up the 'gert hill' from Okehampton. Many of the OPs have been removed, a reminder that nothing stays for long unless there's a preservation group fighting for the cause, and it's unlikely many would wish to champion a cause such as this.

The 1930s was a decade that saw many thousands of people trekking out to the Pool. The Artillery Road now had an improved surface and it meant that cars could more easily reach OP15. It was a lot less of a daunting challenge to only have to walk about a mile to Cranmere in the knowledge that if the Dartmoor weather changed for the worse it wouldn't result in hours of exposure to the elements. This brought people to Cranmere who would otherwise only have ever heard of it in conversation with ardent Dartmoor enthusiasts. Indeed some of the more stalwart wilderness lovers thought that the newly surfaced road made life so easy that 'Cranmere Pool' should be moved to Cut Hill, deeper into the wilds of the upland moors! But there were still those who were more philosophical and those who just got on with the job of getting there from different directions.

Somebody who we have already mentined is Dr Jeffrey Wentworth Malim. Also known as 'Moorover', he lived in St Marychurch, Torquay and was another devotee of Dartmoor. In the summer of 1935 he published his book *The Romance of Dartmoor*, which was dedicated to his three staunch walking comrades – Wealady, Comweal, and Mooroaman. One of my prized possessions is the signed copy that he dedicated 'To Faithful Comweal'. Like many of his contemporaries, he captures the mood and significance of Cranmere Pool.

*To look at Cranmere after reaching it is to search anxiously as though the successful finding was of supreme importance. The attraction lies in its elusiveness, its remote situation in the heart of a morass, at a great altitude, for it is placed at only 150 feet less than the height of High Willhays, the highest point in the south-west of England. In addition to these factors there is an atmosphere of enchantment, woven by the loom of Romance in the minds of many Cranmereans, and this has been encouraged by various descriptive writers and novelists. The finest description of Cranmere is to be found in that fine romance by John Trevenna : A Pixy in Petticoats. Cranmere is not easy to find, as there is no distinctive feature about it…*

*Every route is over rough ground requiring considerable exertion to negotiate, but the nearest way is from the summit of Ockment Hill, by the artillery road from Okehampton. From the roof of Hut 15 the pool may be seen about one mile directly south. It is better not to make a direct line for the pool as the ground is so rough and irregular; rather it is better to bear a little right and gradually descend to the Ockment River, cross it, and follow the stream south-south-east. There is a small branch leading to some rough fen half-way up this little ravine, but it comes in from the east and can be ignored; there is one other little stream to avoid further on, but this comes from the south, so the course is to follow the left branch up the reedy shallow valley where the stream is partly underground. If the route is continued uphill amongst rough peat hummocks, perseverance will be rewarded by arriving at the Cranmere plateau.*

14

However Dr Malim or 'Moorover' wasn't always rewarded for his efforts for on 8 May 1935 there is an entry in his name that states '27th visit, 31st attempt!'

One of the best books that I have ever read about Devon was originally published in 1937 with the title *Under Sail Through Red Devon* written by Raymond B. Cattell. This is an extract, which features just one of many wonderful journeys that Ray did in the mid 1930s:

*On the following day a blazing sun watched the expedition forging again up the East Dart, the broad valley of which sloped upwards interminably towards that lofty plateau on the dome of which lies Cranmere Pool, the highest water in Southern England. A shower-bath under a waterfall gave us renewed energy, though it cost us a copy of* The Times *which Reginald had brought, thinking that if we got lost for some months we should not be without reading matter. Duly separated, it now made excellent bath-towels for four. The leading article we carefully set aside, but unfortunately Pongo* [a dog!] *swallowed it, which is more than most people are prepared to do nowadays.*

*When one emerges on the plateau it is a matter of saying good-bye to the last landmark, in this case the head of the Dart, and faring forth on a great wilderness of bog, cut up by crevasses, which keep one leaping like a frog for several miles. The pool itself is one of several depressions, and is indiscernible from a quarter of a mile's distance.*

*If you approach from the north, Yes Tor will continue to peer at you over the rim of the horizon like a guardian angel until you reach the pool. From Batworthy on the west you may get a compass bearing on Whitehorse Hill (bearing a flag pole on the top) which is exactly east-south-east from Cranmere. But from the south there is nothing until you pick up either of these bearings: you just make a guess and stick to it till you land either at Cranmere or in a bog, or until your memory fails.*

*Whenever Reginald and I get to such a moot point in a moorland expedition, we find it incumbent upon us, as experts, to disagree. The laity present then follows whichever expert looks the more sober. On this occasion, there being nothing to choose between us in the latter respect, they very judiciously divided the angle between the course set between Reginald and myself; so that everyone was satisfied, except Pongo who rushed wildly between the three parties. An open formation is in any case a good plan in finding Cranmere, just as toleration of differences is the only plan which will enable society to reach new goals.*

*The race for Cranmere was now on and the excitement put fevered vigour into our jaded limbs. I had every confidence in the bearing I had taken from the sun and in this confidence I was shortly confirmed by the sight of Reginald, far away to the north-east floundering in a bog.*

*My rivals – Popsy, Jean and Pongo – disappeared over the gently curving horizon a few minutes later, going at a great pace. In the next half-hour I covered a great distance expecting every moment to recognise the jagged hollow of Cranmere, but the expanse of moor remained featureless and desolate except for bogs and crevasses which ever and anon sent me on big detours, panting and cursing.*

*Indeed the next thing I definitely recognised was the hollow of the West Okement River! Bewilderment. By heaven, I had forgotten to correct the bearing by the sun for summer time!*

*I turned and hastened eastward and went on leaping madly from one to another of the giant tussocks of turf which separate the black peat bogs. Presently, I came in sight of the entire party and could see by their wayward rushes that they were not in sight of the goal. The race was not yet lost.*

*Now my heart leapt up at the sight of the hollow with a post in it half a mile ahead. The others saw my spurt and their turning movement brought the watchful Reginald up over the horizon. So he was in the running again, in spite of the bog!*

But the post was only a warning that shells drop here when the artillery is at practice from Okehampton; and now I came across waterlogged shell holes and rusted fragments of shell. What a magnificent thunder the guns make in the hills here! But to-day there will be no barrage to make our goal finally unattainable, for now I sight Whitehorse Hill and no red flag flutters at its mast.

On Whitehorse I got a bearing which had indicated that I had gone practically far enough north. What then had happened? Disillusion was fast setting on all parties and with it exhaustion surged back again. I saw one of the centre party flop. The rest of us wavered, made tentative uncertain sweeps – lost in a featureless desolation. Reginald semaphored an expressive gesture of resignation which I reciprocated by falling flat on my back – "beat to the wide". And then Pongo, who had gone ahead by sheer momentum, not to say doggedness, set up a joyous barking, from some invisible hollow.

He had found the posting box at Cranmere and with it the scent of human beings, after a desert of purely vegetable odours, which, as every dog knows, are scarcely worth smelling.

Thus we came to Cranmere and signed the massive book. Some visitors are evidently so crazed by their hardships that they burst into verse in this book, but the most frequent cry of all is an appeal for a glass of beer, at any price. A vain cry when six miles of trackless moor separate one from the nearest habitation.

Having no letters with us to post and stamp with the Cranmere stamp we had to fall back on the barbaric custom of stamping our chests – a fine tattoo it made – though Popsy, Jean and Pongo refused to receive their decorations.

'Reginald' of this quartet, or quintet if you include Pongo, was the son of the

---

*Map labels:* OKEHAMPTON · Artillery Camp · South Zeal · Yes Tor 2028' · Cawsand Beacon 1799' · Great Links Tor 1906' · Black House · Widgery's Cross · Shell Holes · Walla Brook · Chagford · Cranmere Pool 1900' · Moretonhampstead · Mast on Whitehorse Hill 1974' · R. Tavy · Fur Tor · Merripit Hill 1474' · Postbridge · Widdecombe-in-the-Moor · Great Mis Tor 1765' · Two Bridges · Princetown · Dartmeet · ASHBURTON · 'Pixie-led here' · Wood · Childe's Tomb · Swincombe · Cater's Beam 1543' · Ryder's Hill 1692' · Holne (Charles Kingsley) · Way · Buckfastleigh · R. Dart · Petre's Cross (a great view) · 'Sandpiper' stayed here · Ugborough Beacon 1231' · South Brent · IVYBRIDGE · Miles 0 1 2 3 4

CRANMERE
DARTMOOR
POOL

celebrated Dartmoor expert, Dr Malim.

Vian Smith was another fine writer but one who died years before his time. In his *Portrait of Dartmoor*, first published in 1966, he revealed the pointlessness of making young people go on long route marches.

*Over a hundred years ago it became fashionable to 'do' the tramp to Cranmere Pool …*
*I had the misfortune to be fifteen in the mid 1930s, when hiking was in vogue. Cranmere Pool was suggested to me as a possible motive for being alive … My cry of 'What for?' went unheeded …*

*Those I went with were well equipped … They climbed with a furious energy that appalled me; admiring the view every five minutes because that was part of the treatment, then checking by compass and assuring each other that they were not lost yet. You had to pretend to be lost somewhere on the way. That was good form. Only braggarts and spoil sports made it look easy.*

He also stated some statistics that showed the growing popularity of Cranmere in the early part of the twentieth century for 609 weary wayfarers made it in 1905, whilst the following year, possibly a drier one, saw 962 names recorded there. The trend continued with 1,352 in 1907 and 1,741 in 1908. As computers were not around to catalogue/count them, who sat down and went through the physical process of counting all these scribbles and jottings? We won't demand a recount!

The end of a long Dartmoor winter was marked by another memorable occasion in the annals of Cranmere Pool's history. On Saturday 8 May 1937, 'Cranmere Day', a gathering of invited celebrities, members of the press and general public, met at Cranmere to 'open'

a new box. The idea was the brainchild of Rev. J. P. Baker, Archdeacon of Warrington, who had held previous livings at both Torquay and Plymouth and who had used his time off to explore Dartmoor.

This time the *Western Morning News* were firmly behind the setting up of a more permanent fixture at the Pool. The paper's editor, J. L. Palmer, supported the Archdeacon's idea and 'through the columns of his newspaper' appealed to the populace for funds. These were soon forthcoming and ex-Dartmoor tin miner, Aubrey Tucker, then a sprightly 71-year-old and resident of Sticklepath, was commissioned to build it. He used granite taken from Belstone Tors and used oak for its door. Five men including Aubrey Tucker installed it, the others being Mr J. Newcombe Snr., Mr J. Newcombe Jnr, W. Bennett and A. Crocker.

But it was the other celebrities who were in the limelight that day even though it was, at times, a foggy one. Beatrice Chase, who lived at the hamlet of Venton, a 'suburb' of Widecombe, was among the crowd. In 1925 John Oxenham had written a book and in it dubbed her 'My Lady of the Moor', the book's title. She helped to perpetuate this fictional title by appearing at moorland events. There could not, even in the unusual history of Cranmere, have been many who would have visited the pool wearing a golden wig, with a purple felt hat perched atop it! Although she had promised to maintain a low profile at this event, she had written to many to announce her intended appearance at the ceremony. True to her word she stood at the back of the assembly and cannot be spied in the photographs taken to record the event. Having examined the Visitors' Book, it appears that she didn't sign but quite a few well-known local people did that day.

There were also some notable absentees. The Dartmoor Preservation Association were invited to participate in the event, and that great Dartmoor writer, Richard Hansford Worth, wrote courteously to say that he could take no part. He added, *The Visitors' Book at Cranmere is certainly regarded by most Dartmoor lovers, as opposed to trippers, as being a nuisance. It certainly is wholly inappropriate, and I should love to think there was some way of getting rid of it.* Guess he wouldn't have bought **this** book!

But what of the ceremony that was so beautifully stage-managed by Ruth E. St Leger-Gordon who officially opened the box. Many there were not aware of the sleight of hand that was perpetrated in the sending of the first postcard …

Cranmere Pool

18

This is what Mrs St Leger-Gordon wrote in the *Western Morning News*, on the 25th anniversary of that event, a safe enough span of time having elapsed since her masterful act of deception at the Pool.

*Mr Palmer publicised the event by organising a little inauguration ceremony … the opening to be performed by myself.*

*The arrangement was that after lunching with us in Sticklepath Mr Palmer should drive us up to Splinterproof 15, the usual starting place for the short walk from there to Cranmere. Publicity had brought a spate of of letters to the* Western Morning News *and ourselves enclosing postcards with the request that each may have the distinction of being first to be posted in the new box.*

*Meanwhile, Mr Palmer had suggested that a pleasant gesture would be for me to post the first card to Mr Clive Burn, then Duchy Secretary, making some suitable comment as I did so. Accordingly we wrote the card, placing it on top of the 'first requests' pile waiting to be picked up from the hall table.*

*Unfortunately Mr Palmer was unavoidably late in arriving and consequently luncheon and subsequent departures were very hurried.*

*As we neared Splinterproof 15 we discovered that all the correspondence for postage had been left behind. There was no time to return. Enthusiasts, rain-coated against a typical damp mist, were already trekking Cranmere-wards across the heather.*

*Resort to subterfuge was the only solution. Turning out his pockets Mr Palmer unearthed a battered postcard which he handed to me to make the best of as substitute …*

*The assembly finally gathered round the little hollow. Mr Palmer made a few introductory remarks, Aubrey Tucker (whose 72nd birthday it happened to be) whisked off the flag shrouding his handiwork.*

*I 'opened' the pillar-box, ending my 'speech' mendaciously with the words: "I now have pleasure in posting my first card conveying the good wishes of all present to Mr Clive Burn, the Duchy Secretary."*

*So saying, with furtive sleight of hand, I dropped the fake card (addressed side down) into the letter slit. (Actually I believe Mr Burn was standing unsuspectingly only a few feet away from me.)*

*The problem now was how to abstract the card and replace it with the genuine article, plus all the other would-be 'firsts' before anyone discovered the deception. Cutting short sociabilities, we made an abrupt departure, rattling back to Sticklepath at top speed. The correspondence was snatched from the table, and Mr Palmer and my husband hurtled moorwards again.*

*The former unfortunately was also en route to another engagement in Plymouth and only had time to drop my husband once more at Splinterproof 15, leaving him to effect the substitution, deal with 'any matters arising,' and walk home from there. All of which to our great relief was satisfactorily accomplished somehow without – as far as we know – anyone being the wiser.*

You see, you never know what goes on behind the scenes do you?

The photos of the event show Mrs St Leger Gordon sporting a pair of shoes that were chosen with 'style' rather 'practicality' in mind.

'Cranmere Day' may have been an insignificant event in the history of the world, but it was one that captured the imagination of many and helped to further the reputation of this boggy hollow.

Dr Malim came back the next day to echo what a lot of Dartmoor devotees have thought over the years: *The granite building tones in with its surroundings, is solidly built, of simple*

*design, and unobtrusive, so that none should object to its presence at the Pool.* One might add that it's so unobtrusive that literally thousands have passed by within yards and have failed to find it.

Among the throng that day was S. R. (Reg) Harry, son of Seth Harry, a shop owner from Okehampton who is featured in Mike and Hilary Wreford's *Okehampton Collections I & II.* He must have forged his own route to Cranmere as in the Visitors' Book his name appears with great regularity. It's believed that his first visit to the Pool was in 1897 when he was very young. As he had recorded visit 278 two years earlier – end of April 1935 – he was averaging at least one visit a fortnight!

It's highly unlikely that anyone will ever match, or would want to, S. R. Harry's amazing record of well over 500 visits to Cranmere Pool. On behalf of the *Western Morning News* he took out new visitors' books and deposited filled ones at Plymouth's library. His visits often occurred at the end of the month, for he collected and recorded the rainfall from a rain gauge there. He started this in 1931, a chore that was maintained for several decades. Sometimes the copper receptacle was filled to hernia-threatening proportions, but at other times the sun-kissed moors could hardly raise a dribble. Covering the period 1937-1941, the figures are written in at the back of the Visitors' Books. They reveal a dramatic range of monthly figures. October 1939, a month after the storm clouds of war had broken across Europe, the real meteorological thing broke over Dartmoor and a staggering 22.2 inches was recorded – wet monsoon conditions indeed! By sharp contrast April 1938 could only muster a meagre 0.8 in, veritable desert conditions. If you were to let rainfall statistics rule your decision in planning a dry walk to Cranmere, the wettest months to avoid would be October, November and January. However, Dartmoor weather is so fickle that sometimes mid-winter's day can be warmer than mid-summer's – planning a walking holiday on Dartmoor can be a lottery.

The press accompanied S. R. Harry on the occasion of his 250th visit and a poor reproduction of a photocopied picture is included here, the original, like many old Cranmere pictures, having been destroyed in the Blitz. Mr Harry's 365th visit was also a memorable one and this is what he wrote in the book that day.

*The poet, the philosopher, the fool*
*Are all a bit at sea at Cranmere Pool;*
*Only the mountain sheep, pony and ghoul*
*Can have much fun and games at Cranmere Pool.*

Reg Harry's pilgrimages to the pool were done in all weathers and this in an age when the protective clothing that keeps the worst of the elements at bay today was not yet invented. His only concession to a sudden downpour and consequent drenching was to turn the collar up on his Norfolk jacket and hope for the best. However, twice he had to abandon his car in snowdrifts and he lost count of the number of times in snowy weather when he fell into snow filled crevices up to his waist.

S. R. Harry was an Okehampton man, through and through, and when he wasn't wending his weary way over the moors to Cranmere he was acting as the local registrar for births, deaths and marriages. Reg Harry kept his visits going to the Pool until, when about eighty years old, he fell out of an apple tree! Eddie Hain, also of Okehampton, took over the task of recording the rainfall at the Pool and of replacing full visitors' books.

The Coronation of George VI took place on 24 May 1937 and a rash of entries on

Coronation Day showed that a lot of people used the day off to get away from it all. Therefore visitors to the new box at Cranmere would hardly have found this Dartmoor shrine to be quiet on this momentous occasion! Incidentally had Queen Victoria still been alive, she would have been celebrating her 118th birthday that day but then there wouldn't have been a need for a Coronation.

Mr Harry also was given the task of installing this new stamp on 1 August 1937 on his 386th visit. It was supplied by the *Western Morning News* with the Post Office authorities kindly providing a new inking pad and enough ink to keep this Dartmoor institution functioning. That same year over 200 signatures appeared in the book on one of the Bank Holidays.

In August 1938 the West of England Ramblers' Federation decided that awards should be made to those eschewing the journey to the Pool. The organisation was trying to encourage walkers in the South West to band together in order to improve access and reinstate public rights of way, and saw this as part of an initiative to attract new recruits.

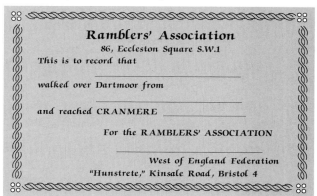

The first hag-hopping hopefuls to claim their certificates were a bit peeved when the written proof of their topographical achievements was not immediately forthcoming and an apology was offered in the *Western Morning News* by the Hon. Sec. of the organisation, Mr Harold Overton. He stated that the first printed batch were not up to the standard required but that suitable supplies of certificates 'worthy of the purpose' would shortly arrive.

The threat of war had been increasing in these years but people got on with their lives and two members of Dobson's Moormen saw in the New Year of 1939 at Cranmere Pool. Their account of their night trek into the wilderness makes an interesting read.

*Saturday, December 31, 1938, was a miserable day, until the early evening, when snatches of moonlight seemed to indicate an improvement. Arriving at Bridestowe about 8.30 pm, we passed Nodden Gate, beyond which is a quarryman's hut a few yards from the Lydford. There we discharged some of our load.*

*Setting out at 9.20, fog or cloud lay well down over the first ridge of high ground, this is from Bra Tor and Arms Tor to Great Links, but not getting disturbed at this sight – fog being less objectionable than rain – we crossed the Lyd and climbed towards Widgery Cross. Soon we removed coats, but not for very long, because we soon reached the floor of the cloud, and found it necessary to don all we had. At the summit of this ridge we were getting it in the neck, the dense drizzle thoroughly damping our gear, but not our intentions.*

*Reaching the Rattlebrook, we crossed the ford which is about two or three hundred yards below Bleak House. The scene was extremely desolate. Now as never previously it was realized the meaning of the Welsh wizard's description of Dartmoor as the 'mist-sodden uplands.'*

*Departing from the track because it was more of a river than track, we next encountered a little difficulty of evading some bog which runs the Green Tor Water. The stretch from*

*Rattlebrook to Amicombe Broad Hole, usually the easiest part of the route in daylight, was found to be the most difficult.*

*The many streaks of deep marsh and springs were thickly covered with ice, and this made the steep descent to the 'Hole' very precarious. Rounding Kneeset Nose, the easier route was followed to Jackman's Bottom, but while crossing this part and looking backward for a moment the impression was nearly sufficient to freeze one stiff, so outlandish and desolate did the surroundings appear.*

*Yet another mile or so of the outward journey remained to be covered, by trudging through the marshy foot of the last-named stream and along near the flooded Ockment. The Pool was eventually reached just after 11.30 pm, or in about 2 1/4 hours from Nodden.*

*The formalities of writing several greetings, stamping them, and signing the Visitors' Book were done in much difficulty. Crouching in thick, soft peat on the edge of the Pool, where it narrows to a gully, and, using for shelter a bank about four feet high, we managed the job, to the accompaniment of rain-drops, of which everything served its quota.*

*The 'Pool' justified its name for once, as there was a considerable amount of water there. Just before midnight the cards were posted, and a record of the occasion obtained in the form of a flashlight photograph of the box.*

*As it was then both another day and a new year, we waived the usual practice of leaving the post for the next arrivals' to remove, and, having retrieved the cards from the box, we began the return journey.*

Since then Bra Tor, possibly named because it was an 'uplifting' experience to climb it, has attracted a bonus letter – t – attached to its ending and is now marked on maps as Brat Tor.

Dr Malim (Moorover) made a similar journey from Bridestowe on a mid-summer's night in 1937. He made it a solo safari and did it without the advantage of a torch, banking on the blessings bestowed by a benign full moon. His 'Midsummer Night's Dream' was complete when he reached the Pool. He had tried a similar stroll on a July night in 1935 but had missed Cranmere when passing clouds eclipsed the moon causing him to flounder fruitlessly in the fen. He then managed to struggle to OP 15 where he slept until a friend came to pick him up just before dawn.

There were several disgruntled visitors to the Pool, in August 1939, when they arrived only to discover the rubber stamp missing. This prompted a stinging letter of anger and disappointment to the *Western Morning News*. After all, they had struggled many miles over the morass only to end up miffed in the mist. But there was a reasonable explanation – our friend S. R. Harry had taken it home to repair it only hours before the frustrated fen walkers had arrived. Mr Harry had taken the stamp, that had fallen apart, had reglued it and placed it in a press overnight. He had returned it the very next day!

Two years is a long time in the life of Cranmere Pool, the daily procession of would-be Cranmereans continuing to take a toll on the poor, much repaired, rubber stamp. By 1940 it was worn out, again, for the umpteenth time. This time a new one was sent to the *Western Morning News* by an anonymous donor from Birmingham.

However that was a minor consideration as for the bulk of the Second World War the letterbox wasn't in place at all as it's believed that a stray shell exploded in its vicinity, sending the box crashing over, leaving it well away from its base.

I have been a keen moorland walker since the age of eleven and there was a period in my late teens, in the second half of the sixties (that is the 1960s!) when I spent much time exploring Northern Dartmoor. Cranmere Pool and its environs were like a magnet to me and my friends and we visited the Pool on many occasions. But what happened to those teenage mindless messages I engraved in the Visitors' Books of Cranmere Pool? Years later, but little wiser, I puzzled about those entries and wanted to have a look at those juvenile entries from my very own 'Wonder Years'.

Plymouth City Library has an excellent 'Local Studies' section that accommodates many of the Visitors' Books for various Dartmoor boxes. These Visitors' Books make compelling reading. The first one at Cranmere Pool served from 1st April (always an appropriate day for the advancement of folly particularly the fenland variety!) 1905 to 16 September 1906. The second was placed there some three days later but was stolen from the Pool on 23 December 1906. Despite offering financial rewards for its return it never re-emerged.

The *Western Daily Mercury* included this on 26 January 1907: *Cranmere, Dartmoor. £2 Reward will be paid to anyone, except the thief, giving information leading to the conviction of persons who took the Visitors' Book from the Pool on Dec. 23rd or 24th. It measured $8^1/2$ by 5 inches and was bound in red pigskin. 'Cranmere, Dartmoor, 1906-1907' was burnt on its edges.*

A poem inside the third volume is dedicated to that thief and goes like this:

*Steal not this book for fear of shame*
*For herein you find the owner's name*
*And when you die the Lord will say*
*Where is that book you stole away?*
*And if you say "I do not know!"*
*The Lord will send YOU down Below!*

At the front of the same volume is the request that people visting Cranmere should collect any postcards deposited there, unless they were from the same day. It was advised they should take the cards and dispatch in the normal way with a note added to say when they were posted on.

There are observable patterns in the penned and pencilled comments of the earliest Visitors' Books to Cranmere Pool, biros or ball points not yet having been invented. Hungarian-born Argentinian, Lazlo Biro (1900-1985) is one of the famous people not to have visited the Pool. However his invention of the ball point in 1944 changed the style of written impressions in the post-war editions of the Visitors' Books.

But the most obvious cry of desperation, in written comments, is for drink and there are numerous promises of wealth offered in exchange for such refreshment. There are many who championed the placement of a drinking fountain in the centre of the pool. And, of course, as the bulk of the visitors were British, there is a stream of comments about the state of the weather. The first recorded foreign visitor in the 1905 edition was a Frenchman on 17 August who used his Gallic charm to fill an entire page.

The other related common comment is always about the ground conditions and expletives, although usually polite, are much in evidence. Many would-be Cranmereans experienced one of those pleasures of life, soaking wet feet whilst en route to the pool.

Perhaps then the hardest thing for all faced with writing something appropriate in the Visitors' Book is to be original. A visitor from the foreign kingdom of Dorset wrote on 2 August 1908:

*I want to write something original*
*But do not know how to begin.*
*There's nothing original in me*
*Unless 'tis original sin.*

Those who scribed on behalf of their pets probably thought they were breaking new ground but a glance through several volumes will throw up paw prints and all sorts of puns about 'dogged' determination in getting there. 'Mowgli' Bowring, a most distinguished visitor (his words not mine), on 6 August 1906, 'wrote': "I got rather wet coming here through the bogs, as I wear no clothes … except a collar. Had a fine time though."

The first drawing to appear in the earliest volume available for inspection was by a Middlesex man, on 30 August 1906, and is reproduced here for your enjoyment and edification. It seems to be the case when anything is tried, even after years, for the first time, it is only a matter of days or even hours before it is either repeated or upstaged. Sure enough, the next page carries a second drawing, revealing what the pool looked like with all its adornments.

In these early volumes it is noticeable that only a small proportion of the entries are in blue or black ink. For some reason there is a lot of green ink and a veritable bloodbath of red although all of these are overshadowed by the humble graphite pencil that is less of a stain devil to clothes and haversacks when of a mind to be mischievous!

The first suggestion, made in a Visitors' Book, for a rubber stamp to be included in the pool's belongings, was made on Monday 22 July 1907 by John H. Strother, Taw View, Belstone: *Reached the pool at 7.10 pm, misty day with cool breeze, and would suggest that a rubber stamp, something like the post office stamps for post-marking letters or rubber stamp for putting the address at the top of a piece of notepaper be provided and kept here. If this were done it would be proof that cards posted had really come from Cranmere.*

Some comments were thus practical and were the seed bed of change but some were designed to be clever. How about this for a gross understatement? C. D. Stubble, of Shilstone House, Throwleigh introduced a friend from London to Cranmere. The old pal's comment was, *It's very quiet, much quieter than London!*

Another party from London, taken into Cranmere's environs in the early 1980s only managed to get a few yards from their car on Okement Hill. Their host quizzed them about their reluctance to continue or even stay for a picnic on the high moor. They told him that they simply could not bear the sound of silence. To them it was an alien experience that they found to be far too eerie for their liking.

Different people derive different pleasures from their open air explorations. For some it's enough to get away from it all, for some to let the beauty or the elements wash over them. For others, though, it is just another opportunity to clock up a statistic. There are many examples ranging from the number of visits made to the pool or the like, the number being more important than the experience or the pool itself. Henry Hodge recorded, with due pride, that he had walked to the pool in precisely one hour and thirty four minutes after alighting

from his train at Okehampton Station. I wonder what kept him!

Others were men with a mission, like John Durant, of Okehampton, who wrote in the book, in November 1918: *Still gathering sphagnum moss for our brave lads who are wounded. Have gathered, carried home, picked over and dried over four tons weight and walked 300 miles. Mr Isaac Sloane, Mr George Smale have also gathered and carried home tons weight.* At that time there was an acute shortage of cotton and the sphagnum moss, although found in inaccessible spots such as the high moors, was light and feathery and a suitable substitute. The vast amount of energy that John Durant used in the quest to gather so much moss took its toll on him and within six years of recording this entry in the book at Cranmere Pool his overworked body finally succumbed.

A little research also revealed that John Durant occasionally used the title 'Lord Cranmere' but only in fun. Born at North Tawton, in about 1863, he worked as a 'gay, sparkling young barman' at his father's hostelry 'The George'. And then one day out of the blue he had a vision and became a devout follower of the Lord. He walked out of the pub and never went back becoming a travelling seedsman with the further nickname – 'The Seedsman Evangelist.'

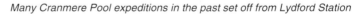

*Many Cranmere Pool expeditions in the past set off from Lydford Station*

He was a popular and jovial man who everyone loved and there was much sadness in the small towns and villages around the moorland edge when he passed away, in 1924, at Okehampton. He lies buried back in his native town with these words of Lewis Court written about him: *In his passing the Dartmoor folk sustained a great loss, but his influence remains as sweet as the perfume of the scented heather on the moorland that he loved so well.*

In the early and middle parts of the twentieth century there was a considerable railway network in place. Many of the people who visited the Pool arrived at the moorland edge by train, this being reflected in their

comments in the book about their direction of approach to Cranmere. The three most popular alighting points for Cranmere Pool appear to have been from the railway stations at Lydford (above), Bridestowe (below) or Okehampton.

The nature of this great upland meant that, in the main, railways had to go around the edge of the moor. Thus anyone alighting at the moorland edge stations had to climb to the heights of Dartmoor – but at least it was downhill on the return journey.

Whatever Cranmere is it certainly shouldn't really be a political place. Charles F. Parker of Freedom Park, Plymouth transgressed in June 1908 when he wrote: *Is it not a real pleasure to be free from the Suffragettes tongue? Why in the name of all that is decent do they not come here and ring that awful bell?* But with plenty of space in the book more political rhetoric followed a short time later. R.

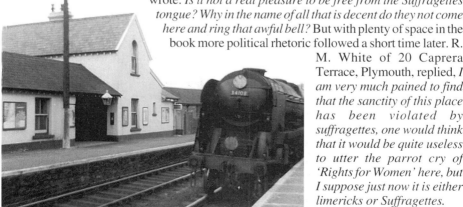

M. White of 20 Caprera Terrace, Plymouth, replied, *I am very much pained to find that the sanctity of this place has been violated by suffragettes, one would think that it would be quite useless to utter the parrot cry of 'Rights for Women' here, but I suppose just now it is either limericks or Suffragettes.*

In those two volumes the majority of people kept their entries to the point but there were those who used it as a platform to air their views and hold forth and consequently the books filled up faster than they needed to have done. Combined with an even greater influx of visitors the Cranmere environment suffered so much so that the next edition of the Visitors' Book, from 19 July 1908, carried the words, 'Please do not waste space' atop every left page and 'Please do not leave bottles, paper etc.' at the head every right one.

Presumably this fell on deaf ears for forty years later nothing appears to have changed...

Eric Hemery's entry in the book for 26 August 1948 stated that he was a member of the Incorporated Society of Musicians. The following year, though, his comment was on a very sour note for on 17 August 1949 he wrote: *I was here two days ago, and it was very badly littered. This morning it was so intolerable that I cleared up and will bury the litter. These revolting litter hounds have no spiritual right on the Moor.* This sort of comment is a recurrent one in most of the Visitors' Books. If walkers have the strength to carry items to the Pool, for consumption there, they should be prepared to take home the packaging that could only, by applied logic, be a lighter, less cumbersome burden!

Initially the advice to save space in the book was heeded but a few 'nonconformists' opened the floodgates and the peat poets came back with a vengeance, scribbling endless renderings.

A 'lost and found' facility was tried at Cranmere in mid April 1935 when L. W. A. Rayner placed the following entry in the book:

*Lost. One R. E. Rayner, medium height, glasses, black hair. If found please return to Exeter as soon as possible.*

But it was not only lost people that were always the problem for the books themselves sometimes went missing.

I tried to discover who visited Cranmere Pool on the day that I was born, purely out of curiosity. I know, for sure, that the Queen didn't, even though she was in the county at the time. She was preoccupied with her duties, as a Princess, opening Princesshay's new shopping precinct in Exeter. Had she been to the Pool, the record of any visit would have been lost as there is a gap, of several pages, between 13 September 1949 and 24 February 1950. The Visitors' Books for the period from September 1950 to March 1961 are missing from the collection held at Plymouth's library and it's unlikely we'll ever know what gems of wisdom were recorded in them.

When the *Western Morning News* severed their association with the Pool, about this time, Eddie Hain continued to supply the books for Cranmere, and some of the other established Dartmoor letterboxes, out of his own pocket, in order to keep the tradition going.

*In 1970 the box was re-sited and re-assembled by a team of dedicated workers, including Eddie and Bryan Hain, Pat Butler, Mike Daniels and Colin Hutchings. (Also involved was Ian Boyes not shown here.)*

The entries for November 1961 include several soldiers from Denbury Camp, near Newton Abbot. This establishment was heavily involved with the setting up of the famous 'Ten Tors' walk, the first expedition having taking place the year before in September 1960 ending at Denbury.

The mid/late sixties Visitors' Book and other more recent volumes are in a far worse state than those from three score years and ten ago. A lot of space has been wasted and some entire pages are occupied with a single boot print. Two different 'Cranmere Pool' rubber stamps are in evidence, one being rectangular, the other being circular but both stating that this mecca in the mire is 1,825 feet above sea level (see page 17).

Sunday, 14 June 1970 was a memorable one in the history of Cranmere Pool. It was also a day English soccer fans might prefer to forget as it was the day the reigning world champions were beaten 1-0 by Brazil in the 1970 World Cup semi-final. As the local team, Cranmere Rovers, whose home pitch is 'iffy' to say the least, were not playing that day, the Royal National Institute for the Blind thought it would be a great opportunity to raise money for their charity by having a sponsored walk to the celebrated Pool. About a thousand pairs of boots and assorted footwear conveyed their respective owners the five miles out along the Artillery Road and off to the soft centre delights of Cranmere country.

Along the way the participants had their wrists stamped as proof of passing certain checkpoints. The sponsorship form was headed something like this:

*THE ROYAL NATIONAL INSTITUTE FOR THE BLIND*
*"THE FIRST CRANMERE POOL PILGRIMAGE"*

*The wildness and beauty of Dartmoor is known to all of us who have our sight and on Sunday, 14th June, Schools and Youth Clubs in Devon, Exeter, Plymouth and Torbay are going to make a Sponsored Pilgrimage, covering a distance of 5 miles, to Cranmere Pool in the heart of Dartmoor, and 5 miles return to starting point by a different route. These young people are doing this to raise funds for the R.N.I.B. ...*

*They realise that these children can never see the beautiful countryside, and they wish to raise money to help this worthy cause ... There is no bar to adults joining in as well if they wish.* The weather was beautiful and a lot of money was raised.

This was to be the first of what was to become a regular event on their calendar but over the years they have varied the route. In 1987 they staged their 'Coming of Age' 18th Dartmoor Celebration Walk and I was invited to write their programme for them and be their special 'guest celebrity' walker.

In later editions of the Visitors' Books it is noticeable that many of the visitors are engaged in marathon walks and a lot of them used Cranmere Pool as a sort of checkpoint on a north/south crossing. This is a long distance route that usually results in walkers having to slog from either Belstone or Okehampton in the north to Bittaford or Ivybridge in the south. Many prefer to do it 'uphill' from the south to the north using the Redlake Tramway to give them a level flying start and the Artillery Road to give them a downhill boost when their bones are most weariest and their legs in need of a little help from gravity.

Many of these stalwart, seasoned strollers like to include the long-established stamps on such a safari. For them Cranmere Pool lies between 'The King of Dartmoor' – High Willhays and the 'Queen of the Tors' – Fur Tor, believed to be the most distant mass from any road. These two important locations are often included in route planning and with a little thought it's possible to include two of the other long established boxes, those of Crow Tor and Ducks Pool.

A week-end camping expedition in late June 1967, on High Dartmoor by young members of the Exeter-based 'Operation Dartmoor' group, proved to be eventful when one of its participants, Chris Parkhouse, fell chronically ill at Cranmere Pool. Later revelations showed that he had experienced a strangulated hernia, a painful problem that was life-threatening in a situation like this. As Cranmere Pool is not noted for its intensive care facilities, M. Ormand and A. C. Howe, better known as Merv and Tony, knew that drastic action was called for.

They decided that the nearest help could be found at Okehampton's Battle Camp about five miles away. Off they went over the hags to Okement Hill and then down the Artillery Road.

Suitably fatigued they arrived at the Camp and raised the alarm. A helicopter was called out from Chivenor, in North Devon, whilst the two lads were taken back as close to the Pool as the army landrover could take them.

The entries in the book show that the party were there at 1.45 am, ten people signing the book. Almost five hours later is a brief entry – *We're still here at 6.25 am – 25 June 1967 (Freezing cold)*. Then, over the page, are a group of soldiers led by Sgt.Swan and Cpl Palk who signed the book at '0935'. The next entry is but five minutes later and tells us of a happy outcome. Or so it would seem. *Helicopter just landed to take Chris to hospital. Raining hard, freezing cold. All the best to Chris.*

Tony Howe had been promised a helicopter trip to hospital to accompany the stricken walker but in the instant he turned around to collect his and the victim's rucksack, he found that it had taken off without him. Today he still remembers that long haul back to Okehampton carrying two heavily-laden backpacks in a way that prevented him from being able to see his feet. If you know the terrain you will know what a tough task this turned out to be. Chris lived to tell the tale. I wonder if Cranmere Pool is his favourite place?

In the 1960s 'Letterboxing' didn't exist as a hobby, as such, for there were only a limited number of boxes to visit. At the end of that 'swinging' decade the list of boxes, with the approximate dates of their origins, was something like this:

*A young Chips Barber atop Johnny Phillips at Cranmere Pool in Jan 1968*

1   Cranmere Pool, 1854
2   Belstone Tors/Taw Marsh, 1894
3   Ducks Pool, 1938
4   Fur Tor, 1948
5   Cuckoo Rock, mid/late 1950s
6   Sittaford Tor, 1959
7   Hen Tor, 1958/59
8   Crow Tor, 1962
9   Childe's Tomb, 1965
10  High Willhays, 1966
11  Bleak House, 1967
12  Cawsand Beacon (Cosdon), 1968
13  Fish Lake, 1968
14  Black Lane Brook, near Ducks Pool, late 1960s
15  Livingstone Waterfalls (Winneys Trough), late 60s. Those 'in the know' will probably be able to cite more letterboxes that were only known by a few.

The location of number 2 in the list may appear to be vague and it might refer to a box that was secreted on raised ground at Taw Marsh, one that was unique in the history of Dartmoor letterboxes. Unlike Cranmere with its thousands of visitors, 'Treasure Trove' was the most elusive box on the moor. This is a flat, poorly drained wet plain in a natural amphitheatre between the bulk of Cawsand Beacon (Cosdon) and the Belstone ridge. It lies below the distinctive and sharp eminence, and a good ol' Dartmoor mountain from this side, of Steeperton Tor. Although it's not known exactly where this box was located, certain details have emerged through the murky mists of time. The box was hidden under a boulder that, despite being exposed to the elements, kept the album protected and it remained in excellent condition for many decades. Its first entry was on 29 August 1894. Inside, at the front of the Visitors' Book was written: *This is Dartmoor's most elusive box. Please keep its exact position a secret.* It was put there by Mrs W. McGillivray of Exeter and the box, over a number of years, accumulated various items of 'treasure' such as copies of national newspapers from 1896, Irish sweepstake tickets, ration book coupons from times of war, tickets of admission to various historic events and a bag of copper coins left 'for our descendants in the 21st century.'

But before you go out treasure seeking you will need to appreciate that this information was gleaned from a newspaper article that was written shortly after the last entry in Treasure Trove's' Visitors' Book in 1949!

Taw Marsh is now an enormous underground reservoir and when the now defunct North Devon Water Board were to embark on major engineering works in this area, the box was lifted until the works were complete. It's believed that the box was relocated in a smart new container but that, too, was many years ago...

So having been distracted by the box that has maintained the lowest profile we return to one that has always been in the public's gaze.

Beyond 1970 there was a steady growth in the numbers of letterboxes to about 40 in 1977. After that an outbreak of boxes became a full scale epidemic with a range of receptacles appearing over and under mire, moor and tor in the 1980s to take their numbers from hundreds into thousands.

And there was also a population boom of 'boxers', strange beings who bestow on themselves like many before them, clever, often moor-related nick-names. Many carry with them their own personal stamps, which presumably cuts down the paper work on arrival at boxes. Their enjoyment of Dartmoor is a very different one from the likes of the Victorians who, unwittingly, were the initiators of this often all-consuming hobby.

Throughout the most recent decades the Artillery Road, that has had so many mentions already in this little book, has been the subject of an enormous amount of debate and controversy. Its upgrading from a rough and bumpy track to a surfaced road about 1930 caused endless arguments with cries from wilderness wanderers to be given a new Cranmere-type shrine nearer to the wilds of Cut Hill or Fur Tor, to make them reach farther out into the moor.

By the same token those who had grown accustomed to having the privilege of being able to drive well onto Dartmoor's highest hills were upset when the road was allowed, in the 1980s, to be allowed to gradually fall back into its original state – a policy referred to as 'Benign Neglect'.

The people of Okehampton, who were probably the major users of this access road, were understandably aggrieved at this and have made their feelings clear to the various authorities involved. However, those who venture along it today should check that their car exhausts are

well anchored and that any other rattly bits will not get shaken off. Dogs (like Dachshunds) with low slung undercarriages, should also proceed along it with due care and attention!

You'll have to formulate your own thoughts as to the whys and wherefores on the emotive subject of what Dartmoor is all about and who it's for and what purpose. Your opinions will probably reflect your own situation – there are always, at the very least, two sides to an argument. Dartmoor has produced some heated exchanges and anything which is debatable has probably been debated about, military use, reservoirs, coniferous plantations, newtakes, letterboxes, the list is endless.

This amazing place called Cranmere Pool is thus something and nothing. Without Perrott's wacky idea, way back in 1854, it is unlikely that many would have ventured into this wilderness of upland Dartmoor. It is probably only the English who would indulge in such pursuits. There are those who celebrate at Cranmere Pool and other similarly strange spots. There have been parties held at OP15, the bunker, or carbuncle, on the Artillery Road. Peter Hodge, from Exmouth, has been involved with parties at Cranmere. The norm seems to be for enthusiasts to don weird and wonderful costumes, grab a totally useless item and meet at the Pool. Mr Hodge has taken such things as electric fires, but presumably only during a heat wave! The spirit of adventure obviously lives on at Dartmoor's most famous shrine.

In getting there a lot of newcomers make the natural mistake of assuming that the large pool of water at Ockerton Court is, in fact, Cranmere Pool and are mystified when the legendary letterbox that they have heard so much about is not to be seen. It's a case of so near but so far for the Pool lies about 1,100 yards (or a full kilometre) away to the south.

One couple, in the 1950s, had been informed about the dangers of this area with the likelihood of sudden mists coming down around their ears to effectively blot out any features of the landscape, not that there are any in this neighbourhood! Lacking confidence in their own abilty to follow a bearing, or even remember the way back to the relative safety of the Artillery Road, they ensured their survival in a most unusual way. Their answer was as simple as the proverbial 'How long's a piece of string?' The answer is about 1,100 yards in this case for our intrepid duo cast caution to the wind to unwind an enormous ball of string from the extensive pool of water at Ockerton Court all the way to Cranmere Pool. Having successfully found their way there they then rewound it on their return journey. It's not one of the normally

*Ockerton Court – **not** Cranmere Pool!*

accepted forms of survival in the great outdoors. I wonder if the couple ever tied the knot …?

Getting to Cranmere Pool is thus an experience that many will remember for a life time. We finish our look at the amazing story of Cranmere Pool with a mild anecdote that epitomises the spirit of the place.

There was a couple of 'old boys' who, when they were young boys, had embarked on that great adventure across the peat fen, all the way to the Pool from Ivybridge. A few years later the friends drifted apart. Both men had qualified in professions that took them right away from the area and more than half a century elapsed before they, accidently, bumped into each other again back in Ivybridge.

By now the once fleet-of-foot lads had moved into that territory of life when such marathon walks, for them, were only done in the mind. One was in his upper nineties and the other, a mere youth, in his lower nineties. Although they recalled, with great clarity, the day of their mammoth march to Cranmere, they couldn't remember the precise date. Their curiosity got the better of them and so they went, with a mission, to the library at Plymouth to consult the Cranmere oracles. They were not to be disappointed and the look on their faces had to be seen to be believed when they found their respective entries in the Visitors' Book. That's part of the enduring magic of Cranmere Pool! Long may it continue!